The Lang Toun

by Jack House

1975

Published by
KIRKCALDY TOWN COUNCIL

Printed by
THE ALLEN LITHOGRAPHIC CO LTD KIRKCALDY

Foreword

by JOHN B. KAY, OBE, JP

The Last Provost of Kirkcaldy

Kirkcaldy - the Lang Toun - has a proud history. That is why the Town Council decided to commission one of Scotland's leading authors to record its story.

The publication of this book marks a watershed in the life of the Town. For centuries it was a Royal Burgh - now the Lang Toun is headquarters of the new Kirkcaldy District, which came into being with the reorganisation of local government in 1975.

It was my privilege to hold the office of Provost during the last years of Kirkcaldy's existence as a Royal Burgh. As a Langtonian born and bred I have an intense affection for the Town, and have long studied its history - but even so, on reading Mr. Jack House's manuscript I found myself learning still more about our Town.

This, of course, is entirely in accord with the comment of Scotland's premier poet, Robert Burns - "Oh, wad some power the gift tae gie us . . . to see oorsels as ithers see us."

I am sure this book will give pleasure to countless thousands of readers in the years to come. One point that I must stress on behalf, not only of my fellow councillors, but also my fellow townsmen, is that 'The Lang Toun' is not Kirkcaldy's epitaph - but simply a record of the life of a community which will go on to greater things.

Contents

1 The Wizard of the North

Once upon a time, as all the best stories start, there was a famous magician in Scotland. He was so famous that he was known throughout Europe as the 'Wizard of the North'. And he was, naturally, a Kirkcaldy man!

Why should I say "naturally, a Kirkcaldy man"? Well, Kirkcaldy is not a big town but it has produced the world's best-known economist, one of Europe's most famous architects, a preacher who had a greater effect than Billy Graham ever had, the founder of *The Scotsman* newspaper, a great explorer, the man who gave the world Standard Time, Admiral Nelson's coxswain aboard the 'Victory', and even the sailor who ran up the immortal signal, "England expects that every man this day will do his duty".

That's by no means the full list of eminent Langtonians and, if you bring in Dysart as well, the roll of honour gets longer and longer, as I shall hope to show you later in this book. Dysart is officially part of Kirkcaldy now, but it's still at heart a separate place, and I must make a bow in its direction.

So it need not surprise you that the 'Wizard of the North' was said to be born in Balwearie Castle, to the west of Kirkcaldy, about the year 1175. His origins and, indeed, a good deal of his life are wrapt in mystery, which is appropriate for a magician. The mystery was heightened by another 'Wizard of the North', Sir Walter Scott, who brought Michael Scott into his *Lay of the Last Minstrel* and even had him crossing the North Sea to bring the 'Maid of Norway' to Scotland. Since this famous voyage was made in 1290 and Michael Scott died around the year 1234, you can see that there's something wrong somewhere. What happened was that Sir Walter mixed up the magician with a later member of the family, Sir Michael Scot of Balwearie, who did go to Norway with Sir David Wemyss of Wemyss on their ill-starred mission.

The wizard himself was a learned man. He was a scholar, a mathematician, a mesmerist, an author, a doctor, and was believed to practise white magic, if not black magic as well. Like many another Kirkcaldy man, he travelled extensively. He went

Kirkcaldy's two most famous sons – Adam Smith *(left)* and Robert Adam.

Below: Gladney House, birthplace of Robert Adam.

to all the important seats of learning in Europe, and the Italian poet, Dante, put him appropriately in his *Inferno* and described:

> "That other there, whose ribs fill scanty space,
>
> Was Michael Scott, who truly full well knew
>
> Of magical deceits the illusive grace."

Michael Scott studied at Oxford and Paris (there were no Scottish universities in his day). He went to Italy and Spain, and taught himself Arabic. For a time he was the official astrologer at the court of the Emperor Frederick II. He translated the works of Aristotle. He was appointed by the Pope of the time as Archbishop of Cashel in Ireland, but he turned the appointment down because he didn't know Irish!

Boccaccio mentioned the 'Wizard of the North' in one of his novels. He referred to "a great master in necromancy called Michael Scot, because he was from Scotland, who received much honour from many gentlemen".

The story goes that, tired of his travels in Europe, the 'Wizard of the North' came back to Balwearie Castle. Not much remains of the castle today and, indeed, you may have difficulty in finding it. Many people, even Langtonians, confuse it with Balwearie Tower, fornenst Balwearie golf course. But the tower, attached to a cottage, is actually a 'folly' and was built by the Fergusons of Raith. If you look up towards Raith House you will see its partner on the top of the hill. 'Follies' were much in vogue in the 18th and even the 19th centuries, and one enterprising firm actually brought out a catalogue of suitable 'follies' for gentlemen, which they were prepared to build. As it happens, these are not the only 'follies' around Kirkcaldy and I'll be coming to the most important of them later in these pages.

To get to the real Balwearie Castle you go up a farm road and, past a now empty mansion and a farm, you come on the remains of Balwearie Castle. Even on a sunny afternoon there is something menacing about it, and it's quite easy to imagine the 'Wizard of the North' coming out of the castle to make a magic circle with his wand on the ground.

Sometimes he invited guests to Balwearie and they sat down to a table groaning with luxurious dishes from all parts of the world. Wonderful wines were served to them. It was only when they got home they realised that they'd had nothing to eat or drink at all. Michael Scott had cast one of his spells upon them and the great dinner was entirely in their imagination.

When wandering beggars came through Kirkcaldy they would go out to Balwearie and the 'Wizard' would come forth to give them food or money. But, if a beggar was unwise enough to say the Christian 'God bless you', the food turned to fire and the coins became withered leaves in their shaking hands.

One day, Michael Scott was returning to Balwearie from Kirkcaldy when he smelt the fine odour of newly-baked bannocks coming from the open door of a farmhouse. He asked the farmer's wife if he could have one, but she said rudely that she had only enough to serve the farm reapers who were expected back at any moment.

Hurt by this discourtesy, the 'Wizard' wrote out a scroll and told his servants to attach it to the farm door. The scroll read:

> "Maister Michael Scott's man
>
> Came seeking meat and gat nane;

An 1840 print of the King's Gait, now Kirkcaldy's High Street.

Below: An old picture of Dysart Harbour.

> So round about the fire I rin,
> With mazled legs and birsled skin.''

As soon as this was done the farmer's wife started to waltz round the fire, which was in the middle of the room. As she danced she shouted the words on the scroll. When the reapers came in from the field they started dancing and shouting too. They were hoarse and tired but they couldn't stop.

The farmer was last on the scene. He was so alarmed by the noise coming from his house that, instead of going straight in , he looked through the window. He had seen Michael Scott and his servant not far off, on their way to Balwearie, and he realised at once that the magician had put a spell on his wife and the reapers. So he ran after Michael Scott and begged him to undo the spell. Michael relented and told the farmer to go to the door, lift the scroll and walk backwards into the house. This the farmer did and immediately the shouting dancers dropped exhausted to the floor.

Everyone knows the ancient couplet:

> ''Some say the Deil's deid,
> And buried in Kirkcaldy.''

Well, it was Michael Scott who finished that particular deil off. This demon attached himself to the 'Wizard' and kept asking him for tasks to do. Whatever seeming impossibility the 'Wizard' demanded, the deil was able to perform it. You'd imagine that an enchanter would be quite pleased to have such a willing demonic servant, but Michael Scott grew tired of the deil's importuning ways.

At last he got a brilliant idea. He told the deil to twist the sands which silted up Kirkcaldy harbour into ropes. Quite joco, the deil went to the harbour and started on the task. But this time he found it was impossible. The failure was so great that he gave up the ghost and disappeared under the Kirkcaldy sands.

What makes this strange story particularly interesting is that a rather more holy tale is told of the Devil in Dysart. I quote from *The Antiquities of Dysart* by the Rev. William Muir, published in 1855.

''There is no doubt'', he writes, ''that our shore has often been the scene of many a rough encounter with the Danes, but unfortunately for the inhabitants of Dysart, a more formidable enemy took possession of one of their caves – this was the Devil. There can be no doubt that they made efforts to eject so dreadful a tenant, and one who doubtless would make himself very troublesome – but the inhabitants of Dysart were too timid to take effectual measures to eject him, or too weak to succeed. What then were they to do ? Fortunately they thought of applying to St. Serf for aid, and sending a deputation to Portmoak imploring the aid of that saint, he is said to have come to Dysart, and ejected the Devil from the cave!''

It's odd that devils should be vanquished in two places so near each other. And, of course, in ancient times saints were supposed to have at least as miraculous powers as necromancers. But it would appear that in this part of Fife you are safer from the 'Powers of Darkness' than anywhere else!

I am more interested in Michael Scott, 'the Wizard of the North', than in the demons. I have a strange feeling that he is still casting his spells. Let me tell you quite frankly that I consider myself to have been bewitched in Kirkcaldy.

When I came to Kirkcaldy to work on research for this book, a Glaswegian friend

A Kirkcaldy street scene of the late 19th century.

of mine said, "Don't be surprised if you find yourself captured by Kirkcaldy. The place has got something about it that's hard to define, but it definitely gets you."

This, to people who don't know Kirkcaldy or who have merely driven through the 'Lang Toun' or maybe just stopped for a meal there, will seem so much nonsense. All that I can tell you is that my Glaswegian friend was so enamoured by the place that he was seriously considering buying a house in Kirkcaldy. And I have met a remarkable number of people from England and from other Scottish towns whose work has brought them to Kirkcaldy and now they don't want to leave it.

I find, too, that the more you see of Kirkcaldy, the more you like the town. On the face of it, it's a straightforward, no-nonsense place, but I detect behind the douce front a romantic strain, a harking back to stirring days and stirring people. Maybe it's because I've been to Balwearie Castle that I can't get the thought of Michael Scott out of my head. I repeat what I have said – 'the Wizard of the North' is still casting his spells.

Balwearie Castle, home of Sir Michael Scott.

Arrowed, in this picture of yesteryear, Kirkcaldy's oldest house.

2 How Kirkcaldy Grew

Sir Walter Scott, the other 'Wizard of the North', was captured by Kirkcaldy and not only put Michael Scott the enchanter into *The Lay of the Last Minstrel* and made Ravenscraig Castle into the Ravenshaugh of *Rosabelle*, but even brought Kirkcaldy into *Rob Roy*. In that novel Andrew Fairservice says, "There's the Kingdom o' Fife, frae Culross to the East Neuk, it's just like a great combined city — sae mony royal burghs yoked on end to end, like rapes of ingans, with their hie-streets, and their booths, nae doubt, and their kraemes, and houses of stane and lime and forestairs— Kirkcaldy, the sell o't is langer than ony town in England."

If Scott thought that in his day, I don't know what he'd make of Kirkcaldy now. Undoubtedly it's still the great place in the Kingdom of Fife, although it may be permitted to doubt if it's longer than any town in England today.

But how did Kirkcaldy start? Nobody can say for certain but in the year 1304 the Abbot of Dunfermline told King Edward, the 'Hammer of the Scots', that King David I of Scotland had given them "a town called Kirkcaldy . . . one of the most ancient burghs in Scotland." And if it was already considered ancient in 1304 it must be very ancient indeed.

Fife was a Pictish kingdom and relics of the Picts have been found in and around Kirkcaldy. There are later relics of the Romans. The position of this place on a bay must have attracted prehistoric people to live there. The first date that puts Kirkcaldy on the map is 596 AD, for in that year, according to one Kirkcaldy historian, occurred the Battle of Raith. It was fought between the Scottish King Aidan and the Angles.

King Aidan was a friend of St. Columba, and maybe he thought he had special protection from the saint. At any rate, the chronicle goes that the King and his royal escort of some 300 horsemen spent a night drinking and at dawn decided to attack the Angles. The King didn't bother to tell the rest of his army, but led his horsemen into the far superior ranks of the invaders. They were simply swallowed up and only three escaped alive.

The Danes were the next to attack Kirkcaldy. They made two big raids in 847 AD

Enlightened architecture has preserved the character of Kirkcaldy's oldest house in a modern setting.

and put Kirkcaldy to the fire and sword. King Constantine led his Scots to victory in the first raid, but in the second he met the invaders at Crail and was killed in battle. King Canute brought a Danish army to Fife in 1035 but was defeated by the Scots led by none other than the Banquo of 'Macbeth'. After that, the chronicler says, the Danes were 'discouraged' and raided no more.

What you might call the first official appearance of Kirkcaldy was in 1075, when the King of Scots, Malcolm III, granted 'the Shire of Kirkaladunt' to the Church at Dunfermline. That is the earliest known spelling of Kirkcaldy, and it was later inscribed as Kircalethin, Kirkaladinit and Kirkaldin. Martin Martin, when he made his celebrated tour of Scotland, suggested that Kirkcaldy meant 'the kirk of the Culdees', one of the earliest of the Christian sects. But nobody believes that now. One likely meaning is 'the town at the crossing place at the mouth of the Den Burn.' But there are other suggestions, and I am not taking sides.

Kirkcaldy belonged to the Church of Dunfermline until 1451, when the Abbot of Dunfermline ceded the land to the town. In 1459 King James II started building Ravenscraig Castle, which is now a picturesque ruin.

It was intended to be a fortress rather than a home for a king. But James II never lived there, for it wasn't finished until 1463 and James had been killed by the bursting of a cannon in 1461.

Despite its several royal associations, Kirkcaldy has always been a very democratic place, and it's a thought ironic to note that, whereas the King's castle is now in ruins, a merchant's house built in the same year of 1459 is still preserved and fulfilling a useful custom. Indeed, custom is the appropriate word because the oldest house in Kirkcaldy, on the Sailors' Walk, is used today as the Custom House.

It's a remarkable place to visit, with its crow-stepped gables, its painted ceilings, and the great Coat of Arms of Charles II, in a wonderful state of preservation. It's said that Charles visited the house when he passed through Kirkcaldy after his coronation at Scone in 1650. Mary Queen of Scots is supposed to have stayed there too, but Mary has been said to have been in as least as many places as her jealous cousin, Queen Elizabeth.

King James V sailed from Kirkcaldy harbour to bring back his Queen from France, and it's surmised he could at least have called at the old house. That was in 1553. In 1559 the Queen Regent, Mary of Guise, brought her French soldiers to Kirkcaldy and they put the town to fire and sword. It's thought that this Mary 'stopped within the ancient walls' of the house in Sailors' Walk.

Well, Kings and Queens were no doubt very important people in their day, but what appeals to me about the oldest house in Kirkcaldy is that it contains at the present details of the ships owned and mastered by local men and signed letters by Adam Smith, a Kirkcaldy man who was much more important than kings and queens. The influence of his book, *The Wealth of Nations*, which he wrote in Kirkcaldy, has gone all over the world, which is more than you can say for Mary Queen of Scots, Jamie the Saxt or even Bonnie Prince Charlie!

The reason for the Adam Smith letters in the present Custom House is that he was appointed to a high position in Customs in his later years. But we'll come to the story of Adam Smith in our next chapter. I can tell you that it's quite an experience

A 1902 picture of 'Bawbee She Kyles' – a game played every New Year's Day near Ravenscraig Castle. Bawbee bets were placed on whether an iron ball could be rolled into one of several holes.

to climb the steep stairs of the old mansion and see the place much as it was away back in the 15th century. It's said that there is a subterranean passage made at the time that the house was an inn, leading to a 'certain hole in the old harbour wall', through which wine and other contraband was smuggled in the days when Kirkcaldy was famous for its smugglers.

If I may jump nearly 200 years, may I remind you that a Pathhead man named Wilson robbed James Stark, the collector of Excise at Kirkcaldy, and was hanged in Edinburgh in 1736. Wilson was a smuggler, but the ordinary people of Scotland supported him, for they found certain laws oppressive and thought there was nothing wrong with smuggling. At any rate, it was the hanging of Andrew Wilson, a baker as well as a smuggler, which caused the notorious Porteous Riot in Edinburgh. It seems that Kirkcaldy has always been in the news!

But I have jumped a wheen of years, and must go back to 1546, when Cardinal Beaton was assassinated. Two Kirkcaldy men were implicated, Sir John Melville of Raith and Henry Balnaves, who was a poet as well as a reformer. Sir John was executed, but Henry Balnaves lived to be a great influence on John Knox.

I've mentioned the time, in 1559, when Mary of Guise's Frenchmen burnt down Kirkcaldy. They were stopped in their depredations at Dysart, when they were faced by the Duke of Argyll and a few hundred men. The two forces looked at each other for twenty days, and then the French lost face and retreated.

When the Reformation came along, Kirkcaldy was strongly for it. The inhabitants were also worried about witches, who always seemed to congregate near the sea. Various people, men as well as women, were accused of witchcraft but Kirkcaldy seemed to take a more enlightened view than those places which either burned their witches alive or drowned them in the sea or the nearest loch or river. In 1604 Dorothy Oliphant was merely 'banished from Kirkcaldy' for being a witch. Other alleged witches were imprisoned. But the only recorded burning of witches alive in Kirkcaldy that I can discover was in 1633, when "Alison Dick, and her husband William Coke" were tied to the stake and put to the flame.

In those days Kirkcaldy had a town piper who received £20 Scots a year. They had also a minister who was said to be the grandson of Mary Queen of Scots and the George Douglas who rescued her from imprisonment in Loch Leven. There were twenty-three salt pans on the beach at Kirkcaldy and the Synod of Fife were worried about Sunday working there. In 1636 the trade of nail-making was started in Pathhead and, as we shall see, this work was to help inspire Adam Smith years later.

The National Covenant for the defence of religious liberty was signed by all the ministers in Kirkcaldy and most of the leading men of the town. Kirkcaldy was strong for the Covenant and the Presbytery of Kirkcaldy made an inventory of arms in the area and supervised the drilling of volunteers. General Leslie was an elder in Kirkcaldy Presbytery and he was appointed head of the Covenanters' army in Scotland. Many Kirkcaldy men joined that army and, when the Covenanters were routed by Montrose at the Battle of Kilsyth in 1645 "that one battle made 200 widows in Kirkcaldy."

More than 400 burgesses of the town were killed in the Covenanters' war, the entire Kirkcaldy fleet of 100 'fine trading vessels' were lost, and the treasures of the town, painfully acquired over the years and sent to Dundee for safety, were seized in 1651

Folly and volley — Nairn's Folly is pictured above,
while below are ranged some 19th century defenders of the realm.

by General Monk of Cromwell's army. Cromwell himself came to Kirkcaldy and lodged in Ravenscraig Castle. As was his custom, he and his men spoiled it when they left.

But you can't keep Kirkcaldy down. Within twenty years Kirkcaldy was the sixth biggest burgh in Scotland and contributed one-fortieth of the whole national tax of Scotland. The burghers were happy to be in such an important town, but they were not so happy about the taxes. They were also worried about the manners of their town. They decided that, "considering many uncouth people and servants come into the town", testimonials should be demanded of incomers. They were worried about weddings. They complained that people who were married on weekdays came into church late and "enter with a gush", and they ordered that "none be married except in clear daylight". They also arranged that a minister, an elder and one of the town's officers should go through the town on Sundays during church services "to observe disorderly persons who are not at church".

Kirkcaldy's fortunes went up and down over the years. In 1688 the burghers made a declaration that "trade is decayed, ships and men lost, and many inhabitants, including magistrates, have deserted the town." In 1715 the Jacobites raided Kirkcaldy and looted the town. The next Jacobite rising, the Bonnie Prince Charlie one in 1745, resulted in Kirkcaldy having to pay tribute of, first, £20, and then £35, which was a lot of money in those days.

But, in the background, things were steadily getting better in Kirkcaldy. Although, in 1760, the Kirkcaldy fleet consisted of one coaster and two ferryboats, within a dozen years it had grown to eleven vessels employing forty-nine men. Various trades had been introduced to the town, notably weaving and the manufacture of stockings. In 1778 Kirkcaldy started building ships and launched thirty-eight vessels in the next fifteen years. Maybe the building of ships was inspired by the danger Kirkcaldy faced when John Paul Jones, called 'the American privateer' in this country and the 'founder of the American navy' in the USA, brought his warships into the Forth and anchored by Inchkeith. This did not daunt the Rev. Mr. Shirra of Kirkcaldy. He went down to the sands and prayed earnestly for the deliverance of the town from the pirates. He had hardly said 'Amen' ere a storm arose and John Paul Jones and his ships were driven out into the North Sea. You can't beat a Kirkcaldy man!

The industrial revolution made a big difference to Kirkcaldy. Cotton spinning was introduced, local shipping increased to a value of £30,000 (an enormous sum in those days), flax spinning came along and there were 2,000 weaving looms in the town, and this coincided with the establishment of Kirkcaldy's first bank, the building of schools and churches, and the establishment of the first Public Subscription Library. Kirkcaldy harbour was greatly extended, with a new pier and wet dock. There was also a new breakwater, but it was destroyed in a storm. In 1846 the railway arrived at Kirkcaldy, and doubtless many of the inhabitants thought that the millenium had arrived.

But bigger things were to come. In 1847 a man called Michael Nairn started to make floor covering. His factory, established in a new building, was known locally as 'Nairn's Folly' by cynical Langtonians. He was so successful that others followed his example, and the time came when Kirkcaldy was known as the linoleum centre of the world.

Curling on Raith Lake in the 1870s.

The manufacture of linoleum was accompanied by a certain smell – of linseed oil, it was said, for linseed was used in the making of linoleum. Kirkcaldy folk were always having their legs pulled about this smell. It was put into song and story. Even the French knew about it, for in 1948 a Parisian publishing firm issued a guide to La Grande Bretagne. This is what the author said about Kirkcaldy:

"Votre odorat vous indequera en temps utile que vous arrivez à Kirkcaldy, qui est le grand centre Ecossais du linoleum. L'odeur du linoleum n'est pas exactement déplaisante, mais elle pénètre et enhavit tout. Ce qui n'empêchera pas, si vous en parlez à un habitant de Kirkcaldy, qu'il ne vous regarde avec surprise et ne vous demande: 'Quelle odeur?' "

In case you don't quite follow, I should explain that the Parisian guide is saying that Kirkcaldy is the great linoleum centre, and that you can tell this by the smell. It's not unpleasant, but it's pervading. If, however, you ask a Kirkcaldy man about the smell, he'll look at you blankly and demand, 'What smell?'

This, I must say, is rather disingenuous on the part of the French guide. Most people in Kirkcaldy, except perhaps the very young ones, remember the famous poem, although they can't recollect much of it except the lines –

> For I ken masel' by the queer-like smell,
> That the next stop's Kirkcaldy.

For the benefit of posterity, I feel the whole delightful series of verses should be preserved in this book. They were called *The Boy in the Train*, and they were written by Mrs. George Smith, a Kirkcudbright girl and daughter of the minister of Mauchline. She wrote the poem for the Merchiston School magazine in April, 1913, and it has been reprinted in a number of anthologies since.

> Whit wey does the engine say toot-toot?
> Is it feart to gang in the tunnel?
> Whit wey is the furnace no pit oot
> When the rain gangs doon the funnel?
> What'll I hae for my tea the nicht?
> A herrin', or maybe a haddie?
> Has Gran'ma gotten electric licht?
> Is the next stop Kirkcaldy?
>
> There's a hoodie-craw in yon turnip-raw!
> An' seagulls! – sax or seeven.
> I'll no fa' oot o' the windae, Maw,
> It's sneckit, as sure as I'm leevin'.
> We're into the tunnel – we're a' in the dark!
> But dinna be frichtit, Daddy,
> We'll sune be comin' to the Beveridge Park,
> An' the next stop's Kirkcaldy.
>
> Is yon the mune I see in the sky?
> It's awfu' wee an' curly,
> See, there's a coo an' a cauf ootbye,
> An' a lassie pooin' a hurly!

You won't recognise him at this distance, but Sir Michael B. Nairn is in the centre of the group in front of this school. It is the Burgh School – also known as the High School, erected in 1843 in St. Brycedale Avenue, Kirkcaldy. The school was included in a government list of 1872 as a 'higher class' school conspicuous by its history and excellent results.

He's checkit the tickets an' gi'en them back,
Sae gie me ma ain yin, Daddy;
Lift doon the bag frae the luggage rack,
For the next stop's Kirkcaldy.

There's a gey wheen ships at the harbour mou',
An' eh! dae ye see the cruisers?
The cinnamon drap I was sookin' the noo
Has tummelt an' stuck tae ma troosers.
I'll sune be ringin' ma Gran'ma's bell.
She'll cry, "Come in, ma laddie!"
For I ken masel' by the queer-like smell
That the next stop's Kirkcaldy.

These charming lines are now completely out-of-date. The 'queer-like smell' is no more, because the making of linoleum is not as big an industry as it was and you can only detect the linseed scent if you are in the place where the linoleum is being made.

And this inspired a Kirkcaldy girl to write a second poem more than fifty years after Mrs. Smith's. She is Helen Brown of Kirkcaldy High School and her verses, entitled *Whaur's the Smell Gaun?*, were printed in *The Scotsman* on November 20, 1965. Here they are —

What's happened tae the queer-like smell
That lingered o'er this toon?
There's no' a trace o' it at a'
Since Barry's works closed doon.
When mist moved in frae aff the Forth
The smell got even worse,
But many an ane would rather sniff't
Than hae an empty purse.

There's naebody wants linoleum noo,
They've a' gaun in fir carpet,
An' a' that's left is a small demand
Frae yon queer foreign Market.
What's happened to oor civic pride?
It's threatened wi' extinction,
Oor Lang Toon is nae quite the same —
We've lost oor auld distinction.

Helen may have been right in her view of things in 1965, but, as I hope to show you later, Kirkcaldy has gained so many other distinctions that the drop in the manufacture of linoleum has been more than compensated for by the new industries brought to the town. Still and all, I know nostalgic people who visit Kirkcaldy's fine Industrial Museum so that they can sniff the 'queer-like smell' once again. There is a special linoleum section in the museum and the scented memory lingers on.

But we mustn't blind ourselves to the fact that other things were happening in Kirkcaldy besides the making of linoleum. In the middle of the 19th century there was a fleet of whalers sailing out from Kirkcaldy harbour. Of the twenty-three vessels

A tragedy and a victory . . . the whaler *Lord Gambier*, lost at sea . . .
and *below* – crowds in the streets of Kirkcaldy on Mafeking Night.

engaged in fishing in the Davis Straits five came from Kirkcaldy. In 1860 three local ships, 'Lord Gambier' 'Chieftain' and 'Abram', had fourteen whales, yielding 200 tons of oil and fourteen tons of whalebone, with a total value of £12,950. Later vessels were the 'Brilliant' and the 'Ravenscraig'.

In those days, too, the town became namely for its schooling, due partly to the beneficence of Bailie Robert Philp, who was a linen manufacturer in Kirkcaldy and left over £70,000 to be used in the education of children. There was even an 'Adventure School' in Kirkcaldy in 1863.

And Kirkcaldy had a Boys' Brigade long before William Smith started the B.B. in Glasgow. In March, 1860, John Thomson started a company called 'Juvenile Volunteers'. He was an ex-superintendent of police and he enrolled some 130 boys between the ages of ten and fifteen. They wore a uniform of trousers with a yellow stripe, a close-buttoned jacket with a standing collar, and a forage cap with an orange band. Their first parade was on Kirkcaldy Sands and the *Fifeshire Advertiser* commented, "That this 'petit' corps is the first of its kind ever formed in Scotland — no small honour to the Lang Toun."

The Juvenile Volunteers were even given two small cannon by Colonel Ferguson, MP, of Raith. So Kirkcaldy's motto, *Vigilando Munio* (They Stand Guard), came true literally.

Kirkcaldy had a 'boys' brigade' before the well-known one was launched.
But this picture, taken in Ravenscraig Park, shows the modern Boys' Brigade on parade.

The group above includes Thomas Carlyle *(second from left)* who taught in Kirkcaldy. Below *(left)* is Michael Nairn — beside him is Bailie Robert Philp, whose generosity helped the town's education programme.

3 Let Us Now Praise Famous Men

When it comes to the listing of the famous men (and women) of Kirkcaldy and Dysart, there's an embarrassment of riches. The selection which follows is mine, and I can only make my apologies to those who find a favourite name missing. But a complete list would take the whole of this book.

We might start with Kirkcaldy's patron saint, St. Brycedale, but there is so much confusion over this name and there is also great doubt as to whether a St. Brycedale ever existed. (He is even said to be a she. with the correct name of St. Bride or St. Bridget). Experts can wrangle to their hearts' content over St. Brycedale, but I take the word of that eminent local historian, Albert Kidd, secretary of the Dysart Trust, that the dedication of the Kirkcaldy Church by Bishop David de Bernham was to St. Patrick, though he could be associated with St. Brisse, Britius or Bricius, and any of these names would be easily corrupted (if that's the word to use for a saint's name) into Brycedale. There are other theories, but Kirkcaldy seems to have settled for St. Brycedale and we shall leave it at that.

The first Langtonian of whom we have any note is Sir John Melville of Raith, an important man during the reigns of James IV and V in Scotland. But he took up the cause of the Reformation and ended by being executed in Edinburgh for treason on December 13. 1548. He was Master of Artillery to the King in 1526. King James V made him Captain of Dunbar Castle, and appointed his son-in-law, Kirkcaldy of Grange, as High Treasurer of the Kingdom. He was obviously riding high in the affairs of State, but he took up the cause of Master Henry Balnaves of Kirkcaldy and that caused his downfall.

Master Henry Balnaves is a man whose name I have seldom heard mentioned in Kirkcaldy but he played a most important part in the history of Scotland. He was born of poor parents in Kirkcaldy in 1502. By the time he died in Edinburgh in 1579 he had become one of Scotland's greatest statesmen. He ranged from such high office as Secretary of State for Scotland in the time of Mary Queen of Scots to imprisonment, as a Reformer, in Rouen.

A famous Raith Rovers football team – see box at end of this chapter.

In Rouen he wrote the first great treatise of the Scottish Reformation. It was smuggled to John Knox, who was then a galley slave in a hell-ship at the mouth of the Loire in France. Reading the words of Henry Balnaves was a turning point in Knox's life. He came back to Scotland and carried through his work on the Reformation with new zeal.

Master Balnaves was not only a friend of the Sir John Melville of Raith who died on the scaffold, but also of his fourth son, Sir James Melville of Halhill. Sir James was a great courtier and courier. He was a Protestant but the friend and confidant of Catholic kings and queens. In particular he was a personal adviser to Mary Queen of Scots and went to London as her ambassador to see Queen Elizabeth. He must have made a considerable impression because, this Kirkcaldy man says, "During the nine days I remained at the Court, it pleased Her Majesty to confer with me every day, in the morning, after dinner, and after supper." We know that the 'Virgin Queen' was very susceptible to good-looking young men, so we can imagine how handsome Sir James Melville was!

Melville was at the Palace of Holyroodhouse on the night that David Rizzio was murdered — indeed, he had warned Rizzio that he was in danger. When Jamie the Saxt, "the wisest fool in Christendom", succeeded to the Scottish throne, Melville was at his side, though he found the King a bit of a bother. Indeed, when the Union of the Crowns took place in 1603, and King James VI of Scotland became James I of England, Melville refused to go with him to London. He said he'd had enough trouble in his life! He left the Court and came back to Kirkcaldy, where he wrote his famous 'Memoirs', and died peacefully at the age of eighty-two.

The next Kirkcaldy man on my list had the distinction of having a book that he had written burned by the public hangman at the Cross of Edinburgh. He was George Gillespie, born in Kirkcaldy on January 21, 1613, His elder brother Patrick became principal of Glasgow University, but their father always believed that the second son would be the better man in the end, though his mother described him as "somewhat dull and soft-like".

Even mothers can be wrong. Young George eventually became "one of the most remarkable geniuses Scotland ever produced". He went to St. Andrews University and became a staunch Presbyterian, so much so that he wrote *Dispute against the English Popish Ceremonies obtruded upon the Church of Scotland*. This was the book burned by the public hangman at Edinburgh.

George Gillespie was a chaplain in Leslie's Covenanting Army. He was minister of Greyfriars Church in Edinburgh before he was thirty, and he made the most important speeches, from the Scottish point of view, at the Westminster Assembly. He was the youngest Moderator ever elected to the General Assembly of the Church of Scotland, but then his health broke down. Suffering from tuberculosis, he came back to Kirkcaldy, hoping that his native air might help to restore him. But it was not to be, and he died at the age of thirty-four.

The 18th century was a time when Scotland produced many famous men and Kirkcaldy did its share. The two most famous were born within five years of each other. They were Adam Smith, the author of one of the most important books in the world, *Inquiry into the Nature and Causes of the Wealth of Nations* (usually

The predecessors of the firemen photographed above were fighting a fire at Pye's factory and as was customary, a representative from the Town House arrived with the subsistence money paid to those men who spent longer than two hours away from the fire station, the money to be spent on food and refreshment. The men felt, however, that something stronger would be appreciated. Indeed it was, but it also impaired their ability to direct the water hoses with any accuracy. By the time the Provost arrived, in answer to an urgent request for his presence, more water was being sprayed on the gathered crowd than on the burning building. The men were sacked on the spot and those photographed above appointed in their place.

shortened to *The Wealth of Nations*, but I thought you'd like to have the original title), and Robert Adam, an architect of universal fame. They went to the same school in Kirkcaldy but, in the way of things in those days, they had to seek fame and fortune furth of the town, although Adam Smith did write the whole of his great book in Kirkcaldy.

Prophets are said to have no honour in their own country, but both these great men have been honoured in Kirkcaldy. In June, 1973, an Adam Smith Symposium was held, with enormous success, in the Adam Smith Centre in the town. Economists came from places as far distant as America and Japan to do honour to the name of Adam Smith. The Symposium was arranged to mark the 250th anniversary of the birth of Adam Smith, and for those who are interested there is an excellently produced book on the meetings.

Robert Adam, whose father and two brothers were also architects, has been remembered this year by a special exhibition of his work in Kirkcaldy, and also by the production of a film entitled *The Hand of Adam*.

Adam Smith was born in the High Street of Kirkcaldy. He was kidnapped by tinkers when he was three years of age, but almost immediately rescued. Apart from that, he lived a douce life. He never married and was the typical 'absent-minded professor'. It's said that he got some of his thoughts for *The Wealth of Nations* from watching the nail-makers at work in Kirkcaldy.

He was Professor of Logic in Glasgow University in 1751 and took the Chair of Moral Philosophy in the following year. He travelled abroad for some years, met many famous Europeans, and came back to Kirkcaldy to write his book. He ended his days in Edinburgh as a Comptroller of Customs. It is recorded that, on the last Sunday of his life, he retired early to his room, leaving his friends at his supper table. "I love your company," he said, "but I believe I must leave you to go to another world." A few days later he was dead.

Robert Adam, though he was always proud of being a Kirkcaldy man, spent more time out of the town than in it. He became the foremost architect in Britain and is buried in Westminster Abbey. When he built a house, he designed everything for it, "from facade to fire irons". He and his brothers leased ground fronting the River Thames and built the famous Adelphi in London. Robert became MP for Kinross-shire. Strange to say, there is not much of his work to be seen in Kirkcaldy, but Edinburgh University and Register House, Hopetoun House and Melville Castle are monuments to his achievement in Scotland.

John Ritchie, the man who made *The Scotsman*, was a Kirkcaldy man. He was born in the town in 1778 and went to Edinburgh in 1801. He was a merchant there, while his younger brother William wrote leading articles and reviews for *The Scotsman*. In 1831 John Ritchie took over the management of the newspaper, and for many years it was printed on a machine made in Kirkcaldy.

Kirkcaldy has produced many remarkable characters, but one of the most remarkable was a little girl who died at the age of eight years and eleven months. She was Marjorie Fleming, known as 'Pet Marjorie' to Sir Walter Scott, who worshipped her. Dr. John Brown, author of *Rab and his Friends*, wrote about her, so did Mark Twain, and Swinburne brought her into one of his poems. A guest of an American President

Street vendors of yesteryear. One provided Langtonians with food for the body, while the bowler-hatted chapman provided food for the mind.

in the White House in Washington found that the only book on the table in the President's private room was *The Story of Pet Marjorie*. And Sir Leslie Stephen wrote about her in *The Dictionary of National Biography*.

Pet Marjorie was born in the High Street, Kirkcaldy, in 1803. She started to write her own style of poetry almost as soon as she could form the letters. It's impossible to give an impression of the lovely artlessness of her verses, but you can read some of them in the Kirkcaldy Museum. The one admired by Mark Twain is about the killing of some turkeys at a farm, and it goes, in part like this. I have kept Marjorie's original spelling, and punctuation.

> Three turkeys fair their last have breathed
> And now this world for ever leaved
> Their Father & their Mother too
> Will sigh and weep as well as you
> Mourning for their osprings fair
> whom they did nurse with tender care
> Indeed the rats their bones have cranched
> To eternity are they launched
> Their graceful form and pretty eyes
> Their fellow fows did not despise
> A direful death indeed they had
> that would put any parent mad
> But she was more than usual calm
> She did not give a single dam . . .

Pet Marjorie was just seven years old when she wrote that. She is buried in Abbotshall kirkyard, and people still make pilgrimage to her grave.

Two men frequently mentioned in any account of Kirkcaldy are Thomas Carlyle, the great author, and Edward Irving, the famous evangelist, but neither can claim to be a Kirkcaldy man. They owe their local fame largely to a Langtonian who was their friend, Patrick Don Swan, Provost of the town for thirty years. Of him it was said, "Mr. Swan's Provostship was one of the most brilliant of her history."

Patrick Don Swan met Carlyle and Irving and the three became friends. Thomas Carlyle was appointed Master of Kirkcaldy Burgh School in 1816 at a salary of £80. Four years before that Edward Irving had been appointed a teacher in a school in Oswald's Wynd, but he gave up teaching for the ministry. Carlyle left Kirkcaldy in 1818 and Irving in the following year, but Irving came back as an evangelist in 1828. Such was his reputation as a spell-binder that the parish church was packed. In the middle of the service the gallery fell and twenty-eight persons were killed.

One of Dysart's far-travelled sons was John McDouall Stuart, who was the first man to cross the continent of Australia. He was born at Dysart in 1815 and his home is being turned into a museum. His name is perpetuated by Mount Stuart in Central Australia. Doubtless in the new museum will be included a McDouall Stuart memento which is already in the Kirkcaldy Museum. It is a piece of the mountain named after him, but it's the second piece sent to Kirkcaldy from Australia. The original one is, at the time of writing, still aboard one of the ships stuck in the Suez Canal!

Another empire builder from the Kirkcaldy district was Sir Sandford Fleming,

Langtonians who lent character to Kirkcaldy in the 19th century — some local worthies on a specially-decorated tram . . . and the Abbotshall Amateur Orchestra of the 1894 season.

born in 1827 at 'Shirra Ha' in Glasswork Street. He was one of the greatest railway engineers of his day and was responsible for the building of many of the long-distance tracks which cross Canada, including the Canadian Pacific.

The Nairn family came into prominence when Michael Nairn started making floorcovering in his 'Folly' in 1847. His son, Sir Michael Barker Nairn, developed the business considerably and gave sites and buildings to the town. In turn, his son continued to assist the welfare of Kirkcaldy and gave Ravenscraig and Dysart grounds to the town.

In 1861 two Kirkcaldy heroes of the Battle of Trafalgar died — William Fair, who ran up the famous signal on the *Victory*, and 'a Pathhead laddie' called Jack Pringle, who was Admiral Nelson's coxswain. And in that same year was born George Langlands, who was town officer of Dysart for fifty-one years and served under eight Provosts — surely worthy of an entry in the *Guinness Book of Records*.

Kirkcaldy and Dysart have been mentioned in books by the brother and sister authors, John Buchan and O. Douglas. They lived in the town when their father was minister of the Free Church at Pathhead. Steps leading down to the sands at Pathhead are supposed to be the origin of John Buchan's *Thirty-Nine Steps*. O. Douglas (Anna Buchan) wrote two novels, *The Proper Place* and *The Day of Small Things* about the Harbour House in Dysart.

Two other Langtonians must be mentioned. One is Joseph Westwood, MP, who became Secretary of State for Scotland. The other is Sir William O. Hutchinson, a fine artist who was director of the Glasgow School of Art, and president of the Royal Scottish Academy.

The famous Raith Rovers team of 1924-25 with the £50,000 forward line, including on right in the front row, the great Alex James. In modern money they would be worth at least £1,000,000.

Queen Elizabeth II visited Kirkcaldy to open the new Town House, centre of the Royal Burgh's administration, and since May 1975 headquarters of Kirkcaldy District Council. Her Majesty is seen with Provost Gourlay.

4 The Neighbours

Kirkcaldy has always been a very individual place, and it may not surprise you, if you have read so far, to discover that it is unique in a democratic sense. I use the word "unique" with due solemnity, and I am willing to do penance in the market place if I am wrong.

The point about the policy of Kirkcaldy as a burgh is that it wouldn't have a Provost. Even today, when burghs are becoming mere districts, there are certain places where the title of Provost, even Lord Provost, will still exist. But, as Kirkcaldy Town Council ends its appointed role, it's worthwhile examining how it all started. And the first thing to be said is that Kirkcaldy, as usual, differed from the rest of Scotland. That's maybe not surprising in an area where they used to say, "Oot o' Scotland and into the Kingdom o' Fife!" But even in the Kingdom, Kirkcaldy stood firm in its resolution to reject a Provost. Away back in the 16th century the burgesses of Kirkcaldy were known as the Neighbours. They assumed the mutual responsibility of the burgesses for the welfare of the town. They might be called ratepayers or electors today, but the terms are not quite the same.

The Neighbours of Kirkcaldy were a strong sodality. They had their own privileges — freedom from oppression, protection against wrongs, rights of trading, and a claim upon the goodwill of the other Neighbours. But in token of these privileges, the Neighbours also bound themselves to take their full share in the community and to defend the rights of Kirkcaldy against all comers.

This meant that it was very difficult for an incomer to become a Neighbour. In practice, it meant that the incomer had either to marry into a Kirkcaldy family or else make a large contribution to the town's funds. You couldn't even stay in Kirkcaldy for a night unless you had been presented to one of the two Bailies of the town and gave your name, what work you did, and what house you were hoping to lodge in.

The Neighbours of Kirkcaldy elected the Magistrates and the Council at the appropriate times. An Act of the Scottish Parliament in 1469 had decided that this right was to be taken away because of the "multitud and clamour of common sympil

A Kirking of the Council — led by the Town Officer. Provost Nicholson, Bailies and Councillors walk through Kirkcaldy's streets to a church service to inaugurate a new council.

persons" — in other words, you and me. This Act ordered that the retiring Council every year should elect the next Council, and that both together should elect the Magistrates.

This was not to the taste of the Neighbours of Kirkcaldy. As far as I can discover, Kirkcaldy was alone in Scotland in refusing to obey the Act. The whole body of burgesses in the Lang Toun agreed to fight it. Here are the actual words of the Resolution against the Provostship. If you take it slowly, I'm sure you will be able to understand it. The point is that it's so much better in the original than in a translation. "22nd April, 1588 —The haill assysse understanding thair is a brute and rumour of sum that monie to seike to be proviest of this burgh, and considdering in cais that purpois tak effect, the same wald be ane perpetuall servitude and slauerie to this toun and nybouris thairoff present and to cum. Tharfor, for preventing of this inconvenience and danger it is thought gud and statut, and ordainit be the foirsaid persons of assyis that na proviest quhatsomever be admittit nor ressavit in na tyme to cum, nor na magistrat be evir heirin chosen, but vnly baillies als of auld use and wont; and quhatsomever nybour or nybouris heirof consentis to the electioun of ane proviest to be chosen, either privatelie or openlie, sall be concludit ane periurit personis, and mansworne aganis the nybouris ayth maid to the toun, and to be depryvat of the freidom of nybourhuid in all time thairafter, and they and thir posteritie to breik ony freidom and libertie within this burgh frae tyme furth and for evir, and als to pay in name of penaltie vnlaw ane hundredth merkis giff he be responsable, and giff they be not responsable of the said soum thai sall be put openlie in the Joggis, the markett dayis, ilk day fra sax houris in the morning to VI houris at evn, but respecting of personis in example of utheris."

The resolution goes on say that the reason for this act is because of the great quietness and stability of the burgh of Kirkcaldy being ruled without a Provost — other towns are under great thraldom and servitude to their Provosts, and there are many other inconveniences in having a Provost. This declaration of freedom was signed by forty of the Neighbours with their own hands, and by a number "with our hand at the notar's pen, becaus we can nocht wreitt ourselff."

There were good reasons for the Neighbours of Kirkcaldy taking this decision. They saw around them cases where a neighbouring laird would get himself elected Provost of a burgh and rule the roost for his personal gain. They stood against this for seventy years, and then in 1658 they elected Robert Whyte as the first Provost of Kirkcaldy. There have been Provosts in Kirkcaldy ever since, with the exception of the year of 1686, when the last of the Stuart kings suspended the elections. Now John B. Kay has the honour of being the last Provost of Kirkcaldy, which has become part of a district in the region of Fife.

Back in 1658 there was a great controversy in Kirkcaldy over the way in which the 'crafts', or trades, were working against the Town Council. So the Provost, Bailies, Town Council, seafaring men, traffickers, merchants, shopkeepers, maltmen and other burgesses and freemen of Kirkcaldy put their case, and the hammermen, wrights, cordiners, tailors, bakers, fleshers and weavers put theirs. The Earl of Rothes was appointed to settle the dispute and ordained that Kirkcaldy Council should consist of twenty-one persons — ten seafaring men, eight traffickers and three craftsmen, with some special privileges for the crafts.

It must not be thought, however, that Kirkcaldy Town Council was a haunt of strife. On the contrary, the powerful Kirk and the strong Council got on extremely well together, particularly in the field of education, which has always been pre-eminent in the thoughts of the Neighbours. They worked amenably together in the establishment of Kirkcaldy Grammar School. But the Kirk gradually opted out of the business of picking teachers and in 1790 the Council examined three candidates for the position of second teacher in the Grammar School. Each had "in the hearing of the meeting to read a page from Milton and one from the 'Spectator', and also sing a tune of music."

One wonders how a modern young teacher would cope with that kind of examination.

In the 19th and the 20th centuries Kirkcaldy Town Council moved steadily ahead. The great controversies of the past were forgotten. Kirkcaldy was a place with the best of all possible worlds. Not only was it successful industrially, but it was also a tourist and shopping centre. The Kirkcaldy Sands were a great attraction to people for miles around. The poem I have already quoted with its refrain, "The next stop's Kirkcaldy" was something very real to holiday-makers.

I have just been looking at the official *Kirkcaldy Guide* for the year 1950. While it pays tribute to the industry of the town, and particularly the sway of linoleum (and brass bands too, when it comes to that!), the guide also suggests that Kirkcaldy is one of the best holiday centres in Scotland.

It says, "Kirkcaldy is a fortunate town in many ways. It has benefited from the great industries started within its boundaries, and it has benefited from being well and wisely run for the past sixty or seventy years. To the original town of Kirkcaldy was added Dysart and other places, and the burgh authorities planned ahead for an increasing population.

"So the municipal services have been steadily improved. An abundant water supply was laid on, new hospitals were built and equipped, the harbour was deepened and enlarged at a cost of more than £100,000, the esplanade was constructed, new roads and bridges were made, and parks were laid out."

To this panegyric was added a couple of years later the words of D. P. Thomson, MA, in his booklet, *Born in Kirkcaldy* – "Boasting a population of approximately 50,000, Kirkcaldy is today the largest town in Fife. With the exception of the cities of Dundee and Aberdeen, it is the most important industrial centre north of the Forth and Clyde.

"Introduced in 1847, by the grandfather of Sir Michael Nairn, Bart., and Sir Robert Spencer-Nairn, Bart., linoleum is the basic industry, but it is far from being the only one. With nine textile factories, three rope works, seventeen engineering establishments, large furniture manufacturing concerns and important printing works, and with a busy harbour and extensive and rapidly developing collieries just on its outskirts, the economy of the town is soundly based."

The authors of the two statements I have quoted had no crystal ball. Mr. Thomson could not know that, within ten years, the economy of Kirkcaldy was in grave danger. The linoleum industry all but collapsed. As for the tourist trade, the famous golden sands of Kirkcaldy were disappearing because of the amount of effluent from the Kirkcaldy coal mines. The town was in a bad way.

But the Kirkcaldy Neighbours are not easily bested. The Town Council formed an Industrial Executive Committee, whose job it was to bring work to the town. I have used the word "unique" for Kirkcaldy before. Now I use it again. This committee was unique, for it was given very unusual powers. It was told to cut straight through red tape, to offer such inducements as houses for key workers and loans for new and incoming industry, and to build two advance factories. Not only was there a national newspaper advertising campaign for Kirkcaldy, but the committee even distributed some 12,000 advertising pamphlets in the first-class carriages of London based trains.

For the record, the names of this remarkable committee should be given. They were Provost H. Alleyne Nicholson, Bailie (now Provost) John Kay, Bailie Alex McLean and Bailie A. M. McMahon, joined by the then Town Clerk, C. D. Chapman, and later the Hon. Treasurer of the burgh, John Brodie.

Their achievements, to put it conservatively, were spectacular. Adam Smith would have been proud of them! But the results of their work belong properly to my final chapter in this Kirkcaldy saga. Since this one has dealt with the growth of a Town Council in Kirkcaldy, it is sufficient to say that few towns have been blessed with such a far-seeing body and so many good servants.

The Lang Toun by the sea . . .

5 Kirkcaldy Today

I find, when I go round Kirkcaldy today, that it's a bright and bustling burgh. It's a happy mixture of sea, town and country and, although it is an industrial centre, it has more pleasant open spaces per head of population than any other town in Scotland – with the possible single exception of Ayr, whose boundaries include a couple of golf courses! Kirkcaldy may well be the only good-sized burgh in Scotland without a slum problem. That's not to say that there is no inferior housing, but what there is appears a small percentage of the total of Kirkcaldy's accomplishments in housing.

Yet I remember visiting Kirkcaldy not so very long ago when a good deal of the centre of the town seemed to consist of "dark, Satanic mills", which cut off the sunlight from far too many streets. But few people in Kirkcaldy objected to them, because they were regarded as the life-blood of the town.

Provost John Kay is quite downright when he says, "In the middle of Kirkcaldy we had five or six eyesores – works surrounded by sub-standard housing. With the contraction of some of our industry, we were able to demolish a number of the works and houses nearby. You can't regard that as anything but good for the town."

This, of course, would *not* be regarded even today as good if it had not been for the influx of new industries to Kirkcaldy and the building of what many people consider the finest local authority housing in Scotland. And that is proved by the number of architectural and other awards which Kirkcaldy has received.

I don't drive a car (having had a stramash with a motor-bike and a barbed wire fence during the last war), so I always go to Kirkcaldy by train. There is a half-hour service from Edinburgh and it's a pleasure to arrive at a modern station, which was given a £100,000 face-lift by British Rail when they saw the way that Kirkcaldy was likely to boom.

Then out of the station into one of Kirkcaldy's parks, the War Memorial Gardens. It's a comparatively small park, but it's perfectly situated with the Kirkcaldy Library and Museum backing it, the Industrial Museum not far away, the War Memorials, the flowers and the walks. I can't think of any other Scottish town where you come out

FLOORCOVERING THEN – AND NOW
. . . The workman on the right is re-enacting
the old method of floorcloth-making –
applying paint to canvas, which was
rubbed down with pumice-stone when
dry, then re-applied until the required
thickness was achieved. *Below* – a picture
taken of floorcloth manufacture about
1880. Pictures on this page and the next
two pages by courtesy of Nairn Williamson.

A modern picture of linoleum maturing in a stove.

Linoleum is only one of the floorcoverings made in Kirkcaldy today. In this picture the manufacture of a modern product, 'Cushionflor', is depicted.

of a railway station into a garden. And, in case you think this is a one-sided view, I should point out that the other exit from Kirkcaldy station leads to a finely landscaped scene, which was once all grey and industrial. Kirkcaldy Parks Department have been known for years as an exceptionally enterprising part of the community activity.

Kirkcaldy's principal library is one of the best I have visited in a middle-sized town. It could do with more space — what modern building of this sort couldn't? — but excellent use is made of what is available, and there is an endearing section for children. In line with modern library tradition, Kirkcaldy's includes not only books and periodicals, but gramophone records, cassettes, tapes and a particularly good photographic section.

Kirkcaldy Museum and Art Gallery is another delight. The art collection is an exceptionally good one for a town the size of Kirkcaldy, and it is famous for its group of paintings by the Scottish artist, Peploe, whose work is much esteemed these days. On my last visit there I was particularly attracted to an exhibition of the Kirkcaldy Potteries, which showed more than 300 examples of pottery work made in the four potteries of the town in the last 260 years or so. Kirkcaldy Links Pottery carried on for something like 200 years and what remains of it now lies under the Raith Ball-room. You'll also see in Kirkcaldy Museum a remarkable armchair carved out of coal by Kirkcaldy miners.

The Industrial Museum is another rewarding visit to make and, as I have said, this is one place where you can recapture the famous 'queer-like smell'. There is, naturally, a special section of the industrial museum devoted to linoleum and it is redolent with scent and nostalgia. There are all sorts of treasures to be found in this museum and even the most romantic people should not be put off by the title 'Industrial'. There is romance in industry too, and Kirkcaldy can prove it.

Across the War Memorial Park I come to the Adam Smith Centre, which has taken a new lease of life since it was rebuilt. To anyone who has not been in Kirkcaldy for years the Adam Smith Centre looks exactly the same as when it was the Adam Smith Halls. But inside it an amazing job of reconstruction has been accomplished. The original building was opened by Andrew Carnegie in October, 1899, and consisted of two halls and a library. The Burgh Architect's Department redesigned the complex to provide a modern auditorium, which can be used for stage shows, concerts or films, a drama studio (which was being used for ballet when I saw it last) known as the Beveridge Suite, and a function suite under the auditorium. The feeling of space inside the Centre is impressive, from the very moment you enter and see the big hall with the floodlit bust of Adam Smith at the far end. It doesn't surprise me to know that delegations have come from various parts of the country to see what has been accomplished in the remaking of the Adam Smith Centre.

I walk down to Kirkcaldy Town House — it's a mere step — and admire its fine facade, worthy of the place where Robert Adam was born. Right on the top of the Town House is a representation in wrought iron of the patron saint of Kirkcaldy, Saint Bryce (sometimes called Brycedale). He is shown in the act of blessing the people of the town in fair weather or foul. Mind you, there's as much controversy surrounding the identity of St. Bryce — even including the suggestion that it should really be St. Bridget! — as there is over the identity of St. Mungo of Glasgow or,

TRANSFORMATION SCENE . . . One of Kirkcaldy's achievements in recent years has been the renovation of the Adam Smith Centre. These two pictures give some idea of the transformation which has taken place. *Below* – the old proscenium arch and stage.   *On the right* – the new foyer.

when it comes to that, of St. Andrew.

Perhaps it's significant that, when you go into Kirkcaldy Town House and see the famous mural facing you, you will not find St. Bryce included among those represented. As you go in, you get this feeling of space that is so typical of Kirkcaldy. The tall mural dominates the scene. It was painted by Walter Pritchard, and it tells you the story of the Lang Toun.

At the foot is Neptune, King of the Sea, with a river figure, bringing trade to the port of Kirkcaldy. Above are arches showing some of the traditional trades of the town — iron-founding, tanning, weaving, coal mining and linoleum making.

On a balustrade above are the Adam Brothers; alongside the renowned architects is the equally renowned economist, Adam Smith; Thomas Carlyle is seen in his Kirkcaldy school on the right. In the classic manner the alcove above shows the figure of Good Government, sculptures of Truth, Justice and Learning, and portraits of Plato, Aquinas and Aristotle.

At the top there is shown the day-to-day life of the town — a young man wooing his lady, a newly married couple, a family scene, a young mother, and an old woman knitting. A figure on a ladder is tending plants, symbol of growth and renewing — and maybe today indicative of Kirkcaldy's welcome preoccupation with open spaces and landscaping.

To one side is a picture of the granting of the Royal Charter to Kirkcaldy in 1644, when it became a free port and did such great trade with the Low Countries. You can compare the dignitaries in the picture with the last of Kirkcaldy's Town Councils.

Provided the Town House remains intact, the painting will last for several hundred years, because the artist used, on a fine quality canvas, an oil paint mixed with a preparation derived from the 15th century.

I walk down into the High Street of Kirkcaldy now, and that's where the bustle is. Kirkcaldy is the chief shopping centre for much of the county of Fife. It's a good mixture of old and new, and the old individual shops are still there alongside the big national stores. Kirkcaldy has one of the finest shopping arcades it has been my fortune to see. From the High Street I walk through it and come out to the esplanade by way of a complex of new buildings, including the fine indoor swimming pool, a hotel and an entertainment centre.

Kirkcaldy Town Council have spent a lot of time and effort in cleaning up the foreshore, though there's not much they can do about the disappearance of the golden sands which once made the town so attractive to holiday-makers. But there is today only one industry on the front at Kirkcaldy. And this part of the town is, to aficionados of the circus and carousel, the place where the largest street fair in Europe is held once a year. Some people claim it's the largest street fair in the world, but we have yet to receive confirmation from Russia about that!

Kirkcaldy Market was fixed as an Easter Chartered Fair as far back as the year 1305. Over the hundreds of years it became a Mecca for showmen in Scotland and other parts of Britain. Now a Links Market runs for three miles along the front and can include forty-five big riding machines, fifty juvenile machines, a couple of circuses, ten shows, and some 370 stalls. There are three times more applications for space nowadays than can be accommodated, and on the day that the positions on the

Langtonians let their hair down at the annual Links Market.

Two more views of the Lang Toun's Links Market — a modern aerial shot . . . and some memories of yesteryear.

esplanade are put up for auction, lots of the townspeople turn out to see the fun. On an average night of the Links Market there can be 100,000 people on the one and a half miles of esplanade.

There are exceptionally good relations between the showmen and the town authorities. All the great showmen's families in this country are represented, and the annual general meeting of the Scottish Showmen's Guild is held in Kirkcaldy during the Links Market, since it is the one time of the year when they are all sure to meet.

Kirkcaldy harbour is always a busy place and is likely to become even busier with the discovery of oil deposits off the coast of Scotland. Opposite the town the Firth is deep and you will almost always see oil rigs anchored for repairs out from the harbour. Large tankers wait in the Forth for the right conditions for sailing to Rotterdam. As Scottish oil becomes more and more important, so Kirkcaldy is bound to be affected to the advantage of the town. What they call nowadays 'oil-related' firms are already interested in acquiring industrial sites in Kirkcaldy, which is exceptionally well placed for that kind of work.

You can go along the esplanade towards Ravenscraig and Dysart. There is a lovely walk along the Firth of Forth by Ravenscraig Park, past the ruined castle. It's remarkable to see how the builders of Ravenscraig made a sea wall to fit the rocks on the sea shore. The wall runs out then in and every now and then there is a sea yett so that you can reach the water. Ravenscraig Park is one of the jewels of Kirkcaldy. The only thing that saddens me about it is that, apparently, the ancient town custom of 'kyling' on New Year's Day is no longer carried out.

This game consisted of rolling an iron ball, actually a cannon ball on loan from Kirkcaldy Museum, towards a round hole cut in the ground. If the ball entered the hole, it was 'kyled'. Bets were taken on the shots and, when a redoubtable player took the cannon ball in hand, his supporters would shout, "A bawbee she kyles!" Later on, of course, the shout was changed to "A penny she kyles!" Unfortunately nobody appears to be kyling at the New Year now, so we don't know what the bet would be in decimal coinage!

From Ravenscraig I walk out to be dazzled by Dysart, which, you soon learn, is not really Kirkcaldy at all, but a much superior place. Well, it's officially part of Kirkcaldy now, and something of a show place, between its ancient buildings, such as the 'Dutch' Town House and St. Serf's Church, and the finely reconstructed old houses on the Sailors' Walk near the Dysart harbour. They have been brought into a scheme of new houses which have been built in the old style, and it's often difficult to tell which is which. You won't be surprised to know that this ancient-and-modern clachan has received architectural awards, notably from the Saltire Society.

Dysart, as I say, still has its harbour, though nowadays it is more namely for yachting and fishing than in the days when it was an important port, trading with ships from Holland, Germany, the Low Country and Scandinavia. Indeed, any good local man will tell you that there is a part of Dysart which is really Norway. The ships from that country used to bring stones as ballast when they came to Scotland. Before they took on a cargo at Dysart, the Norwegians dumped these stones on the shore. There are plenty of them still there and, if you walk among them, you can later tell your friends, quite legitimately, that you have visited a part of Norway.

Kirkcaldy is noted for the high standards of its housing. Here are two modern developments – *(above)* Pathhead; *(below)* Greenloanings.

Another aerial view — and *(below)* Kirkcaldy's swimming pool.

Another pleasant area in which to live – Gallatown; and *(below)*
Raith Housing Estate, which won an architectural award.

I have said so much about linoleum and Kirkcaldy that I feel I should redress the balance, and point out that Dysart has had for a long time a successful carpet industry, being carried on today by the three daughters of the last proprietor.

A safari from Kirkcaldy station to Dysart shore just about does me for a walk, but I have good friends in Kirkcaldy and they take me into the hinterland. Thus I have been able to admire the various housing communities in and around the town. Of the 18,000 houses in Kirkcaldy, some 11,000 have been built by the local authority. The pleasant thing about these housing estates is the apparently never-ending variety of types of houses. There is no effect of the barracks-like building I have seen in some other places I could mention.

It's not surprising in the least that some of these housing estates have won national awards, and, at the last count I heard, more than 250 deputations from other parts of Britain have come to see them. And, for the record, Kirkcaldy had the first major pedestrianised housing estate in Scotland.

A good way to see how Kirkcaldy has developed is to go to Balwearie Secondary School, not so very far from where the 'Wizard of the North' cast his famous spells. It was built in 1964 at a cost of £470,000 and it strikes many visitors as looking rather like a proud ship breasting the waves. It has been described, and justly so, as "one of the educational showpieces of Scotland". From the roof you see a great sweep of the town, ranging from the highly productive Seafield Colliery, with its twin towers, and the lights above Raith Rovers' football ground, over to the beautiful Beveridge Park with the estate of Raith in the background, and across the multi-storeyed buildings of Kirkcaldy.

Incidentally, although Raith Rovers have doughtily upheld the reputation of Kirkcaldy in senior football in Scotland for many years, it shouldn't be forgotten that cricket has always been a principal sport in the Lang Toun. In general, cricket is played more on the east coast of Scotland than on the west, and Kirkcaldy keeps up the tradition.

But we are still on the roof of Balwearie School, and away up there is Kirkcaldy High School, the first school in Scotland to have a language laboratory. It has also swimming pools, a trout and perch pool for biology classes, a completely furnished flat used in teaching housewifery, and a six-lane quarter mile track for the athletes.

There are other fine schools in this airt, but my eye catches Dunnikier Park, once the home of a famous Kirkcaldy family, the Oswalds. Their mansion, in front of which they used to run horse-racing in the season, is now a hotel. Kirkcaldy is the only place I know which has a hotel in the middle of a public park.

You look across the housing estates and the industrial estates. You see the new Technical College, built on the site of the old Kirkcaldy High School. Not far off is one of Scotland's most modern hospitals, the Victoria. The new extension rises to fourteen storeys and cost £2,600,000 in the days when that was a lot of money!

I've visited some of the principal industries of Kirkcaldy too. The town decided, after the world-wide drop in the demand for linoleum, that they would never again depend on one major industry, and so the industries of Kirkcaldy today are as diversified as even the great Adam Smith could wish. Not that linoleum has disappeared. The firm of Nairn-Williamson flourishes and still makes linoleum, al-

Modern housing at Dysart . . . and the bustle of the Lang Toun High Street in 1975.

though that part of the firm's production is comparatively small compared with the output of floorcoverings of all sorts. The company is descended, of course, from the original Nairn one and, although it has very big interests in England, the headquarters have been kept in Kirkcaldy.

I'm not quite sure what the original Michael Nairn would make of the fact that one of the Nairn companies today looks after travel, especially air travel, to and from Scotland and brings Japanese golfers to play in this country and sends Scots to celebrate a Burns Supper in Moscow! I'm pretty sure the original Michael would approve.

I must admit that it surprised me to learn that most of the stage lighting and control equipment for theatres all over Europe is made in Kirkcaldy, Rank Strand Electric at one time spread this work over five factories in different parts of Britain. Now the entire job is done in Kirkcaldy.

Then there's Butler Buildings, who manufacture light fabric buildings which are much sought after by countries behind the Iron Curtain; the Babygro company, whose name explains itself if you think about clothes for children; GEC-AEI Telecommunications, where 3,000 Kirkcaldy women make post office equipment; the Nelbarden Manufacturing Company from Kent; and I must beg the pardon of those firms I haven't mentioned because I simply do not have the space. Still, that will leave you some pleasant surprises when you visit Kirkcaldy and find out that it's even bigger and better than I have boasted.

Three of the older Kirkcaldy industries particularly interest me. Engineering is the longest lasting industry in the town and Fife Forge are still making propellors in Kirkcaldy. Theirs is the only marine engineering shop outside the Forth and Clyde areas. A rather similar industry is the Forth and Clyde Roperie, which was established in the town nearly 130 years ago. Despite its name, it's purely Forth. It was originally run by men from both sides of the country, but some dispute developed and the Clyde men lost their interest. Despite that, one of its most famous products was made by the firm for the Clyde, because Kirkcaldy made the mooring rope for the liner *Queen Mary* when she was launched in the thirties.

The other old industry, though it has moved to one of the new industrial estates, is the furniture firm of A. H. McIntosh, founded in Kirkcaldy in 1869. It has been world-famous ever since then for the production of fine furniture and, even though it is now modernised, it keeps its reputation every bit as high as in the days of the much vaunted Victorian craftsmanship.

Like the Forth and Clyde Roperie, McIntosh helped to supply the liner *Queen Mary* and has made furniture for many other famous ships as well. The modern part I found particularly interesting was where I saw their craftsmen at work, appropriately enough, on reproductions of furniture designs by the much praised Glasgow architect, Charles Rennie Mackintosh. I predict high success for them.

Maybe, after all, that's the reason for the success of Kirkcaldy — the marrying of the old and the new, the keeping of fine traditions, and yet the courageous ventures into the future. Looking back over all that I have learned about the town in writing this study of the place, I'd say that the typical Kirkcaldy man has his head in the air and his feet on the ground. And, could I say hastily, that goes for Dysart men too!

A last look at the Lang Toun . . . from the thirteenth floor of the flats at Pathhead.

Members of Kirkcaldy Town Council and Officials
as at 15th May 1975

Provost John B. Kay, OBE, JP
Bailie William A. Coull
Bailie Rankin G. Grimshaw
Bailie William S. Gibson
Bailie Janet M. Meikle, JP
Bailie Michael Coyne
Bailie Alan H. Potter
Dean of Guild Alexander Wishart
Hon. Treasurer Alexander McLean, JP
Judge of Police Adam I. McMahon
Councillor Grace M. Arnott
Councillor William T. Barclay
Councillor James W. Brodie
Councillor Ferguson Collins
Councillor John B. Cook, JP
Councillor Roy J. Cook
Councillor John Cunningham
Councillor Robert Deas
Councillor Robert Duncan
Councillor William D. Ferguson
Councillor Philip A. Hopcroft
Councillor Frederick J. Hubbard
Councillor Daniel Coyle Leslie
Councillor James McGarry
Councillor Robert McNab
Councillor Jack L. Page
Councillor David Stewart
Councillor Roger P. Strugnell
Councillor John Y. Tarbet
Councillor Sydney Walker

Officials

Town Clerk
James G. Mackay, TD, Solicitor

Depute Town Clerk
R. G. Brotherton, BL

Town Chamberlain
Hugh Wilson, IPFA

Depute Town Chamberlain
Colin Fowler, IPFA, ACIS

Burgh Engineer & Master of Works
G. A. Wood, BSc, CEng, MICE, FIMunE

Depute Burgh Engineer & Master of Works
R. J. Brand, BSc, CEng, MICE

Burgh Architect
D. R. MacGregor, ARIBA, ARIAS

Depute Burgh Architect
J. I. Brodley, DA(Edin), ARIBA

Acting Burgh Planning Officer
Donald Lunan, MA

Director of Social Work
J. E. Thomas, DipSA

Depute Director of Social Work
J. W. Knox, CSW

Burgh Factor
J. C. B. Smith

Depute Burgh Factor
W. Whyte

Sanitary Inspector
John H. Irvine, MRSH, MInstSWM

Depute Sanitary Inspector
R. C. H. Easson

Officials

Parks & Cemeteries Superintendent
Stewart Kirk, FInst, PA(Dip), MInstBCA

Works Manager
Donald W. Swinney, CEng, MIMechE, AMBIM

Depute Works Manager
S. Lofnes, MWSOM, AMBIM

Librarian
Ronald McLaren, ALA

Depute Librarian
Miss Anne Gardner, ALA

Curator
Alexander Hidalgo, BA, FSAScot

Lighting Superintendent
William A. Campbell, FAPLE, MIES

Registrar of Births, Marriages & Deaths
Eston A. Kilgour, LIR

Crematorium Superintendent
Angus T. Coull

Director of Halls & Entertainment
Christopher Potter, BA

Baths Manager
Alexander M. Anderson, MInstBM

Project Co-ordinator
R. D. Bookless, LIOB, AMOMS

Burgh Prosecutor
Austin McLaughlin, MA, LLB

Town Officer
David Aitken